Dare to be Brave

devotionals from the stories of Gideon and Esther

K.J. Bryen

A Note from the Author

The beginning of this book began with me sitting in my old teenage bedroom with a bible in my hand. I had just begun to learn how to overcome my own fears when I studied the stories of Gideon and Esther; I had no idea that it would be the makings of a devotional.

I had never really seen myself as much of a teacher. I have a habit of stumbling over my words when I talk, uttering a series of needless "buts" and "ums." I'd also never written anything like a devotional in my life; fiction was more my forte. I remember asking God, "you really want me to write a devotional? Are you sure?" Several times I tried to swap it for a fiction, but God was firm with me.

When this devotional began to take shape, God slowly began to reveal that the gift of teaching comes in many forms. Since then, God has increased my confidence in teaching, even in speaking. Though I will never be Billy Graham, I've given speeches and taught classes in college with minimal word stumbling, and my devotional writing has improved. I've come a long way. However, this book was the first stepping stone on an unexpected path.

I hope that you discover a new path God has for you from this book; of course, I also hope it will help you dare to be brave!

Sincerely,

K.J. Bryen

Gideon

So the Spirit of the Lord clothed Gideon [and empowered him]; and he blew a trumpet, and the Abiezrites were called together [as a militia] to follow him. ~Judges 6:34

*And the Angel of the Lord appeared to him and said
to him, "The Lord is with you, O brave man." But
Gideon said to him, "Please my lord, if the Lord is
with us, then why has all this happened to us? And
where are all His wondrous works which our fathers
told us about when they said, 'Did not the Lord bring
us up from Egypt?' But now the Lord has abandoned
us and put us into the hand of Midian."*

Judges 6:12-13

Gideon certainly didn't seem very brave when he
talked to the angel about his circumstances. He even
asked the angel why the Lord had abandoned him.
Yet, before Gideon spoke a word, the angel said to
him, "The Lord is with you, O *brave* man."

Gideon didn't act brave when he met the
angel, but God knew his heart. God knew that despite
Gideon's many doubts and fears, he was capable of
great courage. Even more, Gideon was declared to be
brave even while he was afraid!

It's difficult for us to feel courageous in hard
or uncertain times. Fear can manifest in many ways;
fear of an object, fear of a person, fear of failure, or
maybe even fear of doing the right thing because of
how the consequences might affect you. Fear is
natural; we all feel it, even after we are born again.
Gideon was afraid, but even while he was afraid, God
was able to use him in a miraculous way! Even when
we feel frightened, God declares us to be brave. "His
perfect love casts out all fear." In other words, God
has already declared us brave because of His perfect
love. All we have to do is believe His word.

Sample prayer: *"Lord, I'm tired of being afraid of things that I can't change. Please help me to overcome my fear and to trust you."*

The Lord turned to him and said, "Go in this strength
of yours and save Israel from the hand of Midian.
Have I not sent you?"
Judges 6:14

Have you ever had a problem you didn't want to deal
with? One that felt so difficult and beyond your
capabilities, that you just didn't want to face it? If
your answer is yes, then you have something in
common with Gideon. Gideon wanted God to deliver
him from all of his problems. Sometimes, God will
provide a miracle; but most of the time, he asks us to
tackle the problem head on. He wants *us* to be the
miracle.

It's the same principle when it comes to
helping others. Saying a prayer for someone who is in
need is great- prayer is one of the most powerful gifts
God has equipped us with. But before you just pray
for God to miraculously step in, consider whether
there is something you can do to help them. Ask him
to show you if you can do something to help, and He
will give you the ability to do it. God does most of
His work through people. Can you be the tool He uses
to do something great for someone else? God wants
to use you- you just have to be willing to ask.

Sample prayer: *"Father, show me if there's anything I*
can do about the struggles in my life, or to help others
with theirs. If there is, give me the courage and the
wisdom to do it."

But Gideon said to Him, "Please Lord, how am I to rescue Israel? Behold, my family is the least [significant] in Manasseh, and I am the youngest (smallest) in my father's house." The Lord answered him, "I will certainly be with you, and you will strike down the Midianites as [if they were only] one man."
Judges 6:15-16

Have you ever felt like the youngest and smallest in your house- or in other words, like you just can't do anything right? When God calls us, it's easy to say, "Not me, you've got the wrong person, Lord." But God sees every part of you, including your faults. Think about it. Out of 7 billion people in the world, God asked *you* to serve Him. He calls you to come to Him as you are, flaws and all.

Don't let the fear of failure hold you back from doing what God asks you to do. He loves you with an amazing, supernatural love- in fact, God *is* love. No matter how many mistakes you make, He can never stop loving you; that's just who He is. Because He loves you, He will provide all that you need in order to fulfill His divine plan, and He will never leave or forsake you. Just like He told Gideon, He will certainly be with you- and with Him, you can strike down the biggest problems as if they were small ones.

Sample prayer: *"Father, help me to take comfort in your love, and to know that no matter what mistakes I make, you still love me. Help me to be willing to follow the guidance of the Holy Spirit."*

Challenge #1

Strive this week to do something that makes you uncomfortable. It can be volunteering at a homeless shelter, buying a stranger's coffee, or simply offering a friendly hello to someone you don't know. Think about a good thing you can do, then do it.

Overcoming fear usually requires a step out of our comfort zones. Allow yourself to believe that God will take care of you despite the uncomfortable thing you're doing.

When Gideon realized [without any doubt] that He was the Angel of the Lord, he declared, "Oh no, Lord God! For now I have seen the Angel of the Lord face to face [and I am doomed]!" The Lord said to him, "Peace to you, do not be afraid; you shall not die."
Judges 6:22-23

So many times the Bible says, "Do not fear." Yet, so many people today are controlled by it. Conditions like anxiety, social anxiety, depression, bipolar depression, and other psychological conditions are driven by fear. Fear of people, fear of failure, fear of rejection, fear of abandonment. Though conditions should be respected, labels can be dangerous if that person takes it on as an identity. In that instance, they are not seeing it as something that can be overcome, but as a burden to live with.

If we read the Bible in-depth, we see that God can cure any inward pain. It doesn't matter how deep the pain is, or how strong the fear takes hold of us. Faith in God can cure us. It cleanses our minds and makes us whole.

God can pull us out of any pit, if we trust in His love and His grace. This doesn't mean that it will happen right away. Growing in God is a journey, so it may take a long time before you are completely free. However, God doesn't want you to live a mediocre life. Jesus said to "come unto Him, all who are heavy laden and burdened, and He will give you rest." God wants so much for you to access His peace. Lay your burdens on Him today.

Sample prayer: *"Father, thank you for giving me the ability to have faith that can move mountains, and peace that passes understanding. Help me to trust you, and to overcome my fears; to have perfect faith in you."*

Reflections: Overcoming Fear

For most of my life, I suffered from social anxiety. I didn't think of it in those terms for long time, though. Most people just said I was shy or an introvert. While both of those were true, they just didn't seem to capture the full effect that this condition had on my life. I could never really talk to people I didn't know. Every time I tried, I felt tense, and my mind would go blank. I would have preferred being alone rather than attending any event where I would have even had a chance of being put in an awkward situation. I felt fear with almost every invitation extended to me, and with every conversation with a person I didn't know exceptionally well. I second guessed myself on everything I said, and if it even might have sounded awkward, I felt ashamed for the remainder of the day. It even got to the point that when my husband invited his friends over, I would find an excuse to leave the house.

"Social anxiety" began to become a part of my identity. Anxiety was a condition diagnosed by doctors, wasn't it? People don't change medical conditions, they either take medication or they live with them. At least, that was my thought.

After a year working with the same people, I still couldn't talk to my coworkers without feeling that familiar grip of fear, and I started to wonder if this was really something that couldn't be helped. After all, why would God expect me to just live with this condition?

Suddenly, I realized something that changed everything. I'd never actually asked God to deliver me from social anxiety. After many years dealing with my fear, I hadn't even considered to ask my holy creator for help. Once I realized that, I was a little scared to ask- I mean, what if God said no? Still, despite my reservations, I asked God to release me from my social anxiety and, knowing enough to know that belief was the essential to having prayers answered, I allowed myself to believe that He would.

That same day, one of my coworkers began talking to me. As we talked, I could feel the fear stripping off me; all I could think was that it was like the scales from Paul's eyes. The tension in my body released, and I had the longest, most comfortable conversation I'd ever had with a coworker. After that, I was free. Not only was I able to talk to people without fear of judgment, but I made a good friend along the way.

Sometimes the answer to our biggest, most crippling problems is simple. We need to ask God and trust Him to do what we can't. The step to overcoming fear is just to lean on God. Whatever your fear is today, resolve to trust Him. You'll be amazed at what He does in your life!

Challenge #2

Many times, our behavior is actually influenced by the things we say. If we talk negatively about ourselves, our circumstances, or other people, then we not only feel bad, but our negativity spreads to others around us. It steals our joy and our ability to help others.

Next time you are tempted to say something negative, replace it with something positive. No matter how hard your circumstances are, you can always give thanks to God for something good He has done in your life. You may not feel better at first, but if you keep talking positively, eventually you will start to see everything in a positive light.

Now on that same night the Lord said to Gideon, "Take your father's bull, the second bull seven years old, and tear down the altar of Baal that belongs to your father, and cut down the Asherah that is beside it; and build an altar to the Lord your God on top of this mountain stronghold [with stones laid down] in an orderly way. Then take the second bull and offer a burnt sacrifice using the wood of the Asherah which you shall cut down."
Judges 6:25-26

God had just told Gideon that he was going to save his entire people from their oppressors. Gideon may have been thinking, "wow! What a great calling! When do we start?" Instead of sending Gideon straight into battle, however, God asks him to build an altar in His name and to tear down the one his father built that was meant for a false god.

I wonder if Gideon was caught off guard by this. Why not send him to the front lines? Why ask him to do something that seemed totally unrelated- and even more, would incur the wrath of his father and his own people against him?

God has perfect timing. His timing may not always make sense to us. It probably didn't make sense to Gideon, but God knew that he was not ready yet to go into battle, even if he felt called to do it. Gideon needed to have his faith tested first on a smaller scale.

When someone joins the military, they aren't sent immediately into the front lines. First, they have to start with basic training. This time is crucial for them to learn to what to do in times of crisis. It's the same way in our walk with God. God calls us each one of us to our own task for his kingdom; so why don't we get to fulfill this task that we are so passionate about right away? Most of the time, it's probably because we haven't passed basic training yet. God is not going to send you to the front lines until you are fully prepared- He loves you too much to send you before you're ready.

If you are in a time of waiting right now, remember that God sees where you're at. He is the only one who knows what you will face in the future, so He's the only one who knows when you're ready to face it. Pray for the Holy Spirit to instruct and prepare you for your task. Your time will come to fulfill whatever it is God's asking you to do; but first, you have to get through basic training.

Sample prayer: *"Father, thank you for training me to fulfill your purpose in my life. Please help me to be patient as I wait to see that purpose be fulfilled."*

Therefore on that day he named Gideon Jerubbaal, meaning, "Let Baal plead," because he had torn down his altar.
Judges 6:32

Gideon was one of a few people in the Bible who was given a new name after serving God. Before him, there was Abram, who became Abraham. After him, Saul became Paul. It may not seem important, but the changing of a name signifies a change of oneself. It is a reflection of one's new identity in Christ.

Take for example, a couple that gets married. When one person takes the other's last name, it is to signify that they are no longer their own. They belong to their spouse, and are joined to their family. Song of Songs describes us as the bride that enters a divine matrimony with God. When we say "I do," we become a part of His family. From then on, all we can partake in all that He has. But first, we must be willing to let go of our old identity.

We are given a new identity when we give ourselves to God. In place of fearful, we are courageous. In place of weak, we are strong. Instead of a sinner, we are named the righteousness of God in Christ. That means everything before is washed away, and we become a new creature in Christ.

Don't hold onto guilt or condemnation. When God looks at you, he doesn't see junk. He sees the righteousness of God in Christ. We are made anew and blameless in His sight. Yes, *you* are blameless. No matter what sin you have committed, you are already forgiven. You are forgiven, so act like it- receive his forgiveness, and live this new life you were made to live.

Sample prayer: *"Father, thank you that I have new life! Please forgive me of my sins. Help me to believe in how much you love me, and that your mercies are unending. Help me to receive your forgiveness so that I can be a new person through you."*

*So the Spirit of the Lord clothed Gideon [and
empowered him]; and he blew a trumpet, and the
Abiezrites were called together [as a militia] to
follow him.*
Judges 6:34

The Bible is not just a book of rules. It's not a list of
regulations that we can follow to get into Heaven. No
matter what good deeds we do, we will never be
worthy of eternal life. That's why God sent Jesus, so
that we can receive that reward. It's a free gift.
That's also why God sent the Holy Spirit. He guides
us, leading us to God's diving will. He lives in us. He
can give us calmness when we are angry and hope
when we are grieving. He also bestows bravery when
we are fearful. God did amazing things through
Gideon, but only after he was willing to take a step of
faith. That's what the stories of the Bible are about.
It's about regular people taking small steps of faith,
that eventually lead to great victories.

There's nothing you can do to earn God's
love. Every person has sinned, and we're all
descrving of death- but God's mercy knows no
barriers. He sent the Holy Spirit to help us to live the
best lives we can while we are still on this Earth. If
you don't have the Holy Spirit today, pray that you
will receive Him into your heart. If you do this, your
life will be forever changed, and you will never have
to face this world alone again.

Sample prayer: *"Holy Spirit, I accept you into my heart. Please make me into the person I should be. Help me to have faith, and to live the victorious life that you want me to live."*

Reflections: The Guidance of the Holy Spirit

One of the hardest lessons I have had to learn is to allow myself to be led by the Holy Spirit. I'm not always sure when He's speaking to me. Too often, my flesh will counter what the Holy Spirit says, and I'll feel confused.

It's hard, but it's also really rewarding. Here's an example of learning to listen to the Spirit. When I was in high school, I was shy. Like, scared to talk to anyone outside my social group shy. So when I took a class with older students I didn't know, I sat in the farthest corner of the classroom and never said a word.

One day, when the teacher had left the classroom, I heard the other students start a debate about religion. One girl was trying to defend her Christian faith, while everyone else countered her with "facts" to prove her wrong. The poor girl tried to defend herself, but she just didn't know how to respond to the accusations.

Having recently done readings about the authenticity of the Bible, I realized that God had given me answers to every one of the accusations. I felt the Holy Spirit tug on my heart, whispering: "Go."

I froze. *Please don't make me do this,* I thought. But the Holy Spirit said it again: "Go."

I watched as the girl continued to endure the other student's arguments. She stared at them, with no words. I wished I wasn't there. I didn't know if I could bear it. But the Holy Spirit was insistent. Shaking, I got up and sat beside them, then went on to answer their questions with all the knowledge I had obtained from my research. My classmates stared at me in shock. The accusers bombarded me with more "criticisms" of Christian faith, and miraculously, all the questions they asked were ones I had read up on. We debated back and forth until we were left in a stalemate.

I went back to my normal seat after that, and I hardly ever said anything to them again. But I was filled with an overwhelming peace. Were their opinions changed? Did the girl develop a stronger faith because of the knowledge God had asked me to share? I don't know. I do know I did the right thing, and I was filled with a peaceful joy knowing that I had done what the Holy Spirit asked me to.

I could've given into my fear and let them try to convince that girl. I know God would have forgiven me for it, but she also may have been more likely to believe those accusations. That's why the Holy Spirit works through us. We may not always understand what He is trying to tell us. Sometimes, we may even misinterpret what He says. But if we keep trying, if we keep listening and pressing on, the Holy Spirit can help others, through us.

Challenge #3

It can be hard to follow the guidance of the Holy Spirit, especially when we don't seem to be getting anything out of the deal. But doing the right thing always has benefits. Today, ask God to show you how you can help someone else. It can be a scary thing to ask, since it often involves sacrifice. But the blessing you will receive is far greater than anything you might lose. Keep an eye out for someone who you can bless today by God's grace.

*He sent messengers throughout [the tribe of]
Manasseh, and the fighting men were also called
together to follow him; and he sent messengers to
[the tribes of] Asher, Zebulun, and Naphtali, and they
came up to meet them.*
Judges 6:35

When Gideon was in need of support, God sent
messengers throughout the whole region to fulfill His
work. God does not leave you ill-equipped. When He
calls you to do something, it doesn't matter if you
don't have the resources, or the know-how, or the
finances. God is with you; He holds the whole
universe in His hands. He has access to every
resource and He knows all there is to know. If He has
put something on your heart, don't worry about how
it's going to happen. Let Him take care of that. He
has you in the palm of His hand, and He will provide
you everything you need to do His will; sometimes, in
ways you don't expect.

Sample prayer: *"Father, thank you for providing me
with everything I need. Help me to rely on you and to
know that I am well-equipped to face anything the
devil throws my way."*

And the Lord told Gideon, "With the three hundred men who lapped I will rescue you, and will hand over the Midianites to you. Let all the other people go, each man to his home." So the three hundred men took people's provisions [for the journey] and their trumpets [made of rams' horns] in their hands. And Gideon sent [away] all the other men of Israel, each to his tent, but kept the three hundred men. And the camp of Midian was below him in the valley.

Judges 7:7-8

While their enemy lay waiting just below in the valley, God commanded Gideon to send away 22,000 men from his army, leaving him with only 300 soldiers. Gideon had to have been wondering what God was thinking. Why would God ask him to send almost all his men away on the eve of war?

Being brave is not the absence of fear. We all feel fear sometimes. The key to overcoming it is to do something you're afraid to, because it's right. That's bravery. Gideon expressed his fear many times, but he also did what God told him to do. God asked Gideon to send the 22,000 away partly as a test of faith. Gideon probably had a hard time seeing past his circumstance, but because he believed, God rewarded him. They weren't only victorious- they were victorious with only 300 soldiers!

If you feel fear today, remember Gideon. If God was with Gideon despite his fear, He is certainly with you.

Sample prayer: *"Father, help me to be brave like Gideon. When I feel fear, help me to trust you."*

Now on that same night the Lord said to Gideon, "Arise, go down against their camp, for I have given it into your hand.
Judges 7:9

Notice that God didn't tell Gideon, "I *will* give them into your hand." He said they were *already* given to Gideon, before Gideon had begun to advance on the camp.

Stop just praying for your victory. It's good to pray for the things we need, but we also need to recognize that God has already ordained these things to pass. That means they're already yours. If you have accepted Jesus Christ into your life, you have good living on the inside of you from the Holy Spirit. "If you declare with your mouth, 'Jesus is Lord,' and believe in your heart that God raised him from the dead, you will be saved" (Romans 10:9). If Gideon had not believed that the Midianites had been given into his hand, what would have happened to his army? He'd have lost the war before it began.
Do not lose hope today. God is bigger than your problems, and has already given them into your hand. You have victory over Satan- now your part is to believe, and to confess it out loud.

You have victory over your sickness and your finances. You have victory over the people who are coming against, and Satan's attacks on your mind. You have victory over your sin.

Sample prayer: *"Father, although I don't see it, I believe I already have victory over the things I am going through. Thank you for allowing me to be victorious in you."*

When three companies blew the trumpets and broke the pitchers, they held the torches in their left hands, and the trumpets in their right hands to blow, and they shouted, "A sword for the Lord and for Gideon!"
Judges 7:20

Gideon and his men weren't allowed to carry swords into war. The only weapons they had were torches and trumpets. Gideon must have been really confused by this point. God had Gideon sent away nearly all of his men just hours before- now, He tells him to charge onto a large army without a single sword!

Imagine if our President decided to fire all but 300 military men, then sent them to war with no guns. We would be outraged, and there would probably be thousands protesting outside the White House- he could even be impeached for that type of action.

Do you ever feel like the odds are stacked against you? They certainly were with Gideon. Any person watching from the outside would have told Gideon that there was no way he could overcome the Midianites with 300 men and no weapons. In most cases, that person would be right.

Has God told you to do something that seems a little unusual? God is mysterious, and He does not fit into what we would call "normal"- but that's because He knows everything. He sees how everything in our lives fits together into one complete picture, even if all we can see is scrambled pieces of the puzzle.

God can work out every single circumstance for your good. The way He goes about it may surprise you, but if you just trust Him and follow His lead, you will be blessed in the end.

Sample prayer: *"Father, help me to do what you ask, even when it doesn't seem to make sense. Thank you for working every single circumstance for good."*

So Gideon came to the Jordan and crossed over [the river], he and the three hundred men who were with him—exhausted, yet [still] pursuing [the enemy].
Judges 8:4

Gideon and his men were exhausted. Through their fatigue, they had to cross a large river- but they pressed on through their aching legs, their soaked armor, and their tired feet. Although their bodies were screaming at them, they could not let the promise of God slip out of their grasp because of that.

How many times in your life have you not done something God told you to do? If Gideon and his men had given up on the pursuit, they would not have seen God's promise fulfilled that day. If we want to see God's promise fulfilled in our daily lives, we have to be willing to keep our eyes on God while we are exhausted. Even when everything has appeared to go wrong, or the devil is launching a full-scale attack on our minds, we can throw up our hands up and say, "God, I'm tired. The devil is wearing me down; but I also know that you give strength to the weary. Help me to access that strength today- to walk, and not be weary, to run and not faint." Be encouraged today, because God is an expert in rejuvenating weary souls.

Sample prayer: *"God, I'm tired. The devil is wearing me down; but I also know that you give strength to the weary. Help me to access that strength today- to walk, and not be weary, to run and not faint."*

He said to the men of Succoth, "Please give loaves of bread to the people who are following me since they are exhausted, and I am pursuing Zebah and Zalmunna, kings of Midian." But the leaders of Succoth said, "Are Zebah and Zalmunna already in your hands, that we should give bread to your army?" Gideon said, "For that [response], when the Lord has handed over Zebah and Zalmunna to me, I will thrash your bodies with the thorns and briars of the wilderness." He went from there up to Penuel and spoke similarly to them; and the men of Penuel answered him just as the men of Succoth had answered. So Gideon said also to the men of Penuel, "When I come again in peace, I will tear down this tower."
Judges 8:5-9

The truth is, we have all been Succoth and Penuel at some point. Have you ever not offered help to someone who needed it because it was inconvenient, or you thought they didn't deserve it? You may even have felt justified in your actions; Succoth and Penuel did.

Succoth and Penuel missed out on God's best because they weren't willing to help someone. We also miss out when we don't help people. The reason for this is simple: God wants us to have the best lives we can have. If Succoth and Penuel had helped Gideon in his time of need, they would most likely have been rewarded with a strong alliance in Gideon, as well as receiving God's favor. Instead, they had made an enemy of Gideon. Loving people always results in a better life- not just for the people around us, but for ourselves.

Whenever someone needs help today and you find you are tempted to shrink back, step out in faith and lend them a hand. This doesn't mean letting people take advantage of you; ask the Holy Spirit to give you discernment first so that you can recognize when a person really needs help. We are blessed when we help others- *especially* when it feels like an inconvenience.

Sample prayer: *"Father, please give me a spirit of discernment and show me who I can bless today."*

Then the men of Israel said to Gideon, "Rule [as king] over us, both you and your son, also your son's son, for you have rescued us from the hand of Midian." But Gideon said to them, "I will not rule over you, and my son will not rule over you; the Lord shall rule over you."
Judges 8:22-23

Gideon showed humility by choosing not to accept idolization from people. Instead, he got something much better.

Do you ever find yourself seeking the approval of others? We have all done it. We strive to make others like us by impressing them with our successes- but when we finally gain their admiration, it is brief. A few days of praise over our accomplishments, then that praise is passed onto another person. The approval of others is fleeting; the approval of God is eternal.

Ask God to help you to stop trying to please others. Your value is intrinsic; it's not based on the opinion of others. The whole world could hate you, but if you have God's approval, that is worth more than that of all 7 billion people in the world. Ask for help to seek His approval before anything else. If you do this with a willing heart, God may ask you to step out and do some things that make you uncomfortable; but if you do what He asks, you will soon be free from the judgments of others. Instead of insecurity, you will have confidence in God.

Sample prayer: *"Father, I thank you that my value is intrinsic and not based on what other people think of me. Please help me to recognize this and to seek your approval first in my life."*

And the Israelites did not remember the Lord their God, who had rescued them from the hand of all their enemies on every side; nor did they show kindness to the family of Jerubbaal (that is, Gideon) in return for all the good that he had done for Israel.
Judges 8:34-35

Freedom from slavery, the seas parting, food falling from the sky, entering the holy promised land, then deliverance from the Midianites with only 300 soldiers and no weapons- the Israelites witnessed the miracles of God over and over. Yet, they also forgot His help over and over, until they were brought to a place of suffering that made them desperate; only then would they cry out to Him again.

Notice that it was always during the good times that the people forgot God. What stage of life are you going through right now? Are you in the valley? Are you standing on the mountaintop? Perhaps you are somewhere in between? Sometimes on the mountain we forget who brought us there, and we start to believe that it was our own hard work that brought us up. This causes us to judge others who struggle with things that we have already overcome.

If you are in this place right now, you are in a dangerous place. You are building up pride which, when built too high, is often something that God will tear down. Like the Israelites, you will be brought back deep into the valley so that you might once again cry out to God.

However, if you are in the valley right now, know that God uses our suffering to bring us closer to Him. "And we know that in all things God works for the good of those who love him, who have been called according to his purpose" (Romans 8:28). You might not understand why you are suffering, but God does. If you continue to praise Him, He will lift you back onto a mountaintop.

"For those who exalt themselves will be humbled, and those who humble themselves will be exalted" (Matthew 23:12).

Sample prayer: *"Father, please help me to praise you and to give you everything I have- no matter what season of life I'm in."*

Esther

". . . And who knows whether you have attained royalty for such a time as this [and for this very purpose]?"~ Esther 4:14

Now when it was each young woman's turn to go before King Ahasuerus, after the end of her twelve months under the regulations for the women—for the days of their beautification were completed as follows: six months with oil of myrrh and six months with [sweet] spices and perfumes and the beauty preparations for women— then the young woman would go before the king in this way: anything that she wanted was given her to take with her from the harem into the king's palace.

Esther 2:12-13

When chosen to be considered as the future queen, Esther had to wait for twelve months before she could even meet her potential husband. She probably found the anticipation to be excruciating; but this period of time was essential for her to prepare to meet the king.

That's how God deals with us sometimes. He reveals a great plan for our lives, and we are excited to start it- then He makes us wait. That wait can be so hard! God wouldn't ask us to wait it weren't for a good reason, though. If God had let Esther meet the king unprepared, she wouldn't have fulfilled her purpose. Waiting is the time we can prepare for what God has called us to do, and learn some patience while we're at it. If you're waiting for something to happen in your life, ask God to bring it to pass in His perfect timing. For all you know, He might be using this time to prepare you for your destiny.

Sample prayer: *"Father, help me to enjoy the journey just as much as I look forward to the end."*

Reflections: A Lesson in Waiting

When I was saved a second time at age twenty, I had no idea what God had in store for my life. I wanted to know right away what God had in store for me! Instead, He made me wait almost a full year to find out what my next step should be in life.

I was impatient at first. I tried lots of different paths in hopes that God would support me. My plans ranged from becoming a journalist to opening up my own animal rescue. However, I felt frustrated every time I took a step towards these things. I wrote fiction during this time that, looking back, were my worst pieces of literature. My plans failed, and I didn't understand why. After eight months of trying and failing, God showed me why they weren't working out: because they were my plans, not His.

I learned to be content not knowing what His plans were after that, and I finally found joy in what I was already doing. I wasn't looking far into the future; I was finally seeing what was right in front of me. Only then was I ready for Him to reveal His plan to me.

I could still be rushing off chasing my own ideas if I had never stopped and listened to God. If you aren't sure what God wants you to do- just wait. God is preparing you, and when you are ready, He will reveal His purpose. It's the journey to where we're going that makes us who we are.

"I am not saying this because I am in need, for I have learned to be content whatever the circumstances. I know what it is to be in need, and I know what it is to have plenty. I have learned the secret of being content in any and every situation, whether well fed or hungry, whether living in plenty or in want. I can do all this through him who gives me strength."
-Philippians 4:11-13

*Now the king loved Esther more than all the other
women, and she found favor and kindness with him
more than all the [other] virgins, so that he set the
royal crown on her head and made her queen in the
place of Vashti.*
Esther 2:17

Esther was blessed with being in the right place at the
right time. God gave her favor with others, and that
allowed her to not only win the king's heart, but to
save her people from destruction.

I wonder how many tragedies each of us have
been spared from due to divine intervention? Do you
frequently complain about your job or maybe your
house? God may have you there for a reason. God
could have placed you in your workplace to be a light
to the people there. Your house may need work, but
perhaps God is using those issues to prepare you for
things coming in your future. God places us exactly at
the right place and at the right time, if we will follow
His lead- but we have to be willing to give up what
we want, and let Him use us for a better purpose.

Ask God to give you favor, and to fill you
with the Holy Spirit so that you can follow His lead.
You are chosen by God, He loves you, and He wants
to give you your best possible future. All you have to
do is to surrender yourself to His will, and then ask
(see Matthew 7:7).

Sample prayer: *"Father, please bless me with your
divine favor. Help me to surrender myself to your
plan, even if I don't see the whole picture yet. Help
me to be a light where I am at."*

Challenge #4

Do you ever want to ask God why you are where you are right now?

    . . . Then why haven't you?

    Jesus said, "Ask and it will be given to you" (Matthew 7:7). God won't be offended if you ask Him for answers. If you find yourself wondering what the right thing to do is, just ask. God doesn't want us to just pray on Sunday mornings and Wednesday nights. We should be in constant communication with Him. He wants to be involved in every single detail of your life, from your major aspirations all the way to how you fix your hair in the morning. Nothing is too big or too little to God. In fact, even our biggest problems are tiny in comparison to Him!

    If you are wondering what is the next big step for you, ask. If you just want to know whether you should go to the grocery store tonight or if you should wait, ask. Start the habit today of talking to God about everything. God loves you, and He wants to walk beside you in everything- but He won't force Himself on you. First, you have to ask.

Esther had not revealed her family or her people [that is, her Jewish background], just as Mordecai had instructed her; for Esther did what Mordecai told her just as when she was under his care.
Esther 2:20

Esther was asked to keep a secret not only from her husband, but everyone else too. That must have been difficult. Yet, she was obedient out of respect for Mordecai, who she knew was a man of God.

So often we rush through our daily lives, going from errand to errand; then at the end of the day, we wonder where our day went. We focus on being done with the task, and forget to enjoy the moment.

Have you ever been asked in an interview, "where do you see yourself in five years?" That can be a very difficult question to answer because we struggle to see beyond our immediate future. It can be so hard to see past what is going on around us.

The reason we can't see our entire future is because it would overwhelm us- but God sees it, from beginning to end. You don't have to know the ending. Esther probably didn't understand why she should keep something so big from nearly everyone in her life, and she might have wondered when the secrecy could finally come to an end; but God saw the beginning to the end. He knew it wasn't the right time because if she waited to reveal her heritage at the right moment, that revelation could save her people.

Has God asked you to do something that seems difficult, and you've found yourself wondering why? Take heart, because your circumstance doesn't surprise God. He knew it was going to happen, and He knows what will happen in the future. So don't worry about where you are at right now or where you will be. God will take care of it, if you just trust Him enough to let Him take the lead.

Sample prayer: *"Father, help me to trust you with my circumstances, even when I don't understand what's going on."*

Reflections: Obeying when you don't Understand

When I was high school senior, I was so excited to go off to college. Still, I didn't know what university to go to. After many campus tours, I asked God if He had a preference on my college and my major. I heard the still, small voice of the Holy Spirit almost instantly.

"Choose any college, but bring me with you wherever you go. Major in anything, except don't major in music."

I remember looking up at the ceiling with my face scrunched in confusion, and thinking towards God, *what does* that *mean?*

I loved music, and I had considered majoring in vocal performance. Why would He tell me not to major in something I loved? And how could He not have a preference on my university?

He didn't answer me that day. So I did as instructed, and chose a college myself, making sure not to choose music as my major. The college I chose turned out to be an incredible experience, and it is where I met my husband. As for my major, I majored in History, but tried over and over to pursue music opportunities along the way. Practically every music opportunity fell through somehow, and it confused me every time. I didn't get why God would want to keep me from doing something I loved.

Years after I'd already graduated from that university with a B.A. in History, I was singing in my car, as I normally did during my commute to work and back. As I was singing, something hit me that I'd never realized before: I wasn't trying to glorify God with my singing. I was singing to glorify myself.

This realization completely changed music for me, and from then on God began to teach me how to sing for His glory. As soon as I began to learn how to sing for Him and not me, I was presented with a few actual music opportunities. He inspired me to write songs, I became part of the musical worship team at my church, and I got a gig for the first time. Suddenly, I was singing not for myself, but for Him; that was God's intention all along.

This musical journey with God has been a blessing, but it took several years for Him to provide me with a full answer to why I had to take a break from music. If God tells you to do something that is confusing, so long as it doesn't contradict scripture, trust that He has your best interests in heart. If it's God telling you to do it, then it can only be good for you in the end.

All the king's servants who were at the king's gate [in royal service] bowed down and honored and paid homage to Haman; for this is what the king had commanded in regard to him. But Mordecai [a Jew of the tribe of Benjamin] neither bowed down nor paid homage [to him].
Esther 3:2

We must make the decision every day to either do what's expected of us by others, or to do what we know is right.

Doing what's right can be so difficult when we crave the approval of others. While its normal to want good relations with others, it can be easy to cross that threshold into being a people pleaser. Being a people pleaser is different from putting others before yourself. A people pleaser will neglect their own needs simply for the approval of others, and even worse, they might ignore God. The bible clearly says that a man pleaser cannot please God.

Mortdecai chose what was right by not bowing down to Haman, but after doing the right thing, he and all of the Jews became in mortal danger. Doing the right thing seemed to only increase his problems.

Sometimes doing the right thing seems to backfire on us. It was already hard enough to make the right decision, and then it's like it only makes things worse; but God has a plan. God sees what you did, and He sees the end from the beginning. While you may not yourself see it, He sees the blessings that are coming your way.

If you believe you have teetered the line of being a people pleaser, simply ask God to help you to seek His approval before that of people. However, if you have already done the right thing in spite of others, and it has brought on hardship, take heart. Jesus did the right thing every day of his life, and he also suffered greatly; but he said he has overcome the world. God provides joy throughout every hardship. Take heart throughout your trials and tribulations, because Jesus has already overcome the world.

"I have told you these things, so that in me you may have peace. In this world you will have trouble. But take heart! I have overcome the world." -John 16:33

Sample prayer: *"Father, help me to seek your approval before that of people. Help me to do the right thing, no matter the consequences."*

*Now it happened when they had spoken to him day
after day and he would not listen to them, that they
told Haman to see whether Mordecai's reason [for
his behavior] would stand [as valid]; for he had told
them that he was a Jew.*
Esther 3:4

Do you immediately try to argue when someone
challenges your faith?

Mortdecai chose to not say anything.
Have you ever heard the phrase, "If you can't say
anything nice, don't say anything at all?" Mortdecai
knew that explaining himself to those men wasn't
going to sway them. Taking a defensive stance would
have only stirred them against him, and he probably
would have been tempted to sin in his anger.
Mortdecai had the wisdom to discern that the
situation called for silence over words.

Be aware that some people who question your
faith with a hostile attitude may just be trying to stir
up strife. Paul often warned churches against letting
strife develop; strife pollutes our relationships, and
spurs us to commit sin out of anger. Strife reigns in
useless arguments and short tempers.

When you're with a person who's trying to
stir up strife, keep your peace. God may ask you to
speak gentle words so as to melt their heart. Other
times, He may show you it is better to be silent.

Sample prayer: *"Father, help me to keep my peace in
strife, and give me the wisdom to know when I should
speak and when I should be silent."*

Then Mordecai told them to reply to Esther, "Do not imagine that you in the king's palace can escape any more than all the Jews. For if you remain silent at this time, liberation and rescue will arise for the Jews from another place, and you and your father's house will perish [since you did not help when you had the chance]. And who knows whether you have attained royalty for such a time as this [and for this very purpose]?"
Esther 4:13-14

Mortdecai believed that God would deliver him and the Jews whether Esther helped them or not, even though there was no deliverance in sight. He just wanted to see it done through Esther so that she would be blessed.

Walking in faith is simply trusting God to handle our situations. How would the world change if Christians lived with this kind of faith on a daily basis? When others see our faith (especially during difficult times), they may begin to desire that for themselves. Our faith is a light to others; but when we lose faith during our hardships, it hurts our testimony.

Hardships are painful, and when we go through them we don't feel like praising God; but God asks us to look beyond our feelings. Even when we are hurting, we have the choice to lift our hands up and surrender that hurt to God. He may not show you the way out immediately- but take heart, because problems are always temporary. Your pain will pass. So take His hand, and let Him walk with you through it. You never have to be alone.

Sample prayer: *"Father, please help me to believe like Mortdecai. Help me to surrender my life to you."*

Reflections: Living Supernaturally

Since I began my walk with God, He's asked me to do many things I didn't want to. These things were always very difficult to get beyond, even though I knew the result would be good.

I had one of those moments at church one Sunday when God asked me to offer a comforting hand to a man who was hurting. I didn't know the man well. Though I knew God was telling me to do it, my own logic held me back. I thought, *the man doesn't know me, he probably doesn't even want my comfort,* and, *what if he thinks I'm crazy?* I finally asked God why I couldn't seem to bring myself to do it. I heard Him respond:

Because you are living in the natural, not the supernatural.

The answer surprised me, but I quickly realized He was right. Obeying the Holy Spirit meant believing in something I couldn't see, and trusting that God would guide me. It meant believing in the supernatural.

Having faith is pretty much all God asks of us; if we have faith that He is real and He sent His only son to die on the cross for us, then we will naturally want to keep His commandments. However, having faith also means you need to stop looking at the natural, and live a supernatural life.

Esther and Mortdecai had this faith. They stepped out of their comfort zones. They put their lives and everything they had at risk, and they were blessed because of it. God protected them when they were afraid and allowed them to do great things for Him, all because they decided to believe in the supernatural.

Ask God to help you with this type of living. Pray that you will stop relying on this natural world, and start having faith in the supernatural promises of God.

*On that night the king could not sleep; so he ordered
that the book of records and memorable deeds, the
chronicles, be brought, and they were read before the
king. It was found written there how Mordecai had
reported that Bigthana and Teresh, two of the king's
eunuchs who were doorkeepers, had planned to
attack King Ahasuerus (Xerxes). The king said,
"What honor or distinction has been given Mordecai
for this?" Then the king's servants who attended him
said, "Nothing has been done for him."*
Esther 6:1-3

There is a chronicle of deeds that exists; greater, longer, and more accurate than the King's. This is God's chronicle, which holds the deeds of every single person who has lived on this Earth.

Such a chronicle would be terrifying if it included all our deeds, good and bad. However, over 2,000 years ago, Jesus gave us an eraser. Because of what He did, God is willing to erase every bad deed as if it were never there. Even more exciting, God remembers all the good ones!

When we sin, we should repent with a pure heart and receive His forgiveness- then move on. God has erased the sin from our chronicle, and so meditating on what we have done only makes us miserable. It's not holy to feel guilty all of the time; it indicates that you don't really believe that God forgives you.

Think about your chronicle of deeds. Do you see the good you have done through God's grace, or are you focusing on the bad? Do you truly believe that He has given you an eraser for your life?

Sample prayer: *"Father, please forgive me of my sins. Help me to receive your forgiveness and to live the abundant, joyful life you want me to have."*

So Haman said to the king, "For the man whom the king desires to honor, let a royal robe be brought which the king has worn, and the horse on which the king has ridden, and on whose head a royal crown has been placed; and let the robe and the horse be handed over to one of the king's most noble officials. Let him dress the man whom the king delights to honor [in the royal robe] and lead him on horseback through the open square of the city, and proclaim before him, 'This is what shall be done for the man whom the king desires to honor.'" Then the king said to Haman, "Quickly take the royal robe and the horse, as you have said, and do this for Mordecai the Jew, who is sitting at the king's gate. Leave out nothing of all that you have said."

Esther 6:7-10

"God opposes the proud, but shows favor to the humble." -James 4:6

When comparing Haman and Mortdecai, Haman desired praise from people, while Mortdecai only wanted favor from God. Ironically, Mortdecai was the one who got the praise that Haman desired.

Do you ever desire recognition from others? It's natural to want to be appreciated every once and a while; but where humans fail, God appreciates you. Appreciation from people is fleeting, but God's favor is eternal.

If you learn to humble yourself before God, He will exalt you at the right time. However, you first need to let go of the need to be exalted. Ask God for humility in your life. If you currently have a problem with pride, God may have to bring you down a peg like He did Haman- but if you submit yourself to Him, He will lift you back up.

If you can recognize pride as soon as it begins, it will be easier to put a stop to it before it takes root in your heart. Being humble also puts you in a better place to help people. It's easier to help others when you're looking at eye-level, rather than looking down.

Sample prayer: *"Father, help me to be humble, and show me how to prevent pride before it begins."*

*In it the king granted the Jews who were in every city
the right to assemble and to defend their lives; to
destroy, to kill, and to annihilate any armed force that
might attack them, their little children, and women;
and to take the enemies' goods as plunder, on one
day in all the provinces of King Ahasuerus, the
thirteenth [day] of the twelfth month (that is, the
month of Adar).*
Esther 8:11-12

When the order was given to wipe them out, there
wasn't any visible evidence that the Jews would be
saved; but God rescued them just in time. He didn't
strike down their enemies for them. Instead, He gave
them power to fight their enemies. We Christians
sometimes ask for miracles to make our problems go
away. Most of the time, God doesn't make our
problems disappear- He gives us the power to deliver
ourselves.

God never promised an easy life; quite the
opposite, in fact. Jesus said that in this world, there
would be trouble, but to take heart! He has overcome
the world (John 16:33). With Him carrying us, we
don't have to fear.

Think on the gift He has given you with his
spirit. God, gave you power- *His* power. You have the
power of the creator of the universe gifted to us by
the Holy Spirit. No problem in this world is too big
for God. He is right beside you, and you can
overcome anything that comes against you.

Sample prayer: *"Father, show me how to access your power in my life. Help me to believe that with you, I can handle anything that comes my way!"*

Then Mordecai departed from the presence of the king in royal apparel of blue and white, with a large crown of gold and with a robe of fine linen and purple wool; and the city of Susa shouted and rejoiced.
Esther 8:15

Notice that Mortdecai got received recognition and blessings, but only after going through difficulties.

Every one of us experience obstacles daily; sometimes they can seem so big, that they bring us to our knees. God is watching, and He sees our pain. We may not always understand why things happen, but God picks us up. He picks us up off of the ground so that we can stand. You may not understand why, but God does; He already sees the blessing at the end of this difficulty.

This life isn't all there is. There's so much more than awaiting than what's in front of us. Heaven has many mansions, and we each have our own room reserved, so take courage knowing that God is with you. He will carry you through every trial if you let Him, and you will be rewarded if you stay faithful. Like Mortdecai, you will not only be delivered- you'll be stronger than you were before.

Sample prayer: *"Father, help me to submit to your will, and to let you carry me when I go through trials. Give me strength and help me to keep my eyes on you."*

At the citadel in Susa the Jews killed and destroyed five hundred men, and [they killed] Parshandatha, Dalphon, Aspatha, Poratha, Adalia, Aridatha, Parmashta, Arisai, Aridai, and Vaizatha, the ten sons of Haman the son of Hammedatha, the Jews' enemy; but they did not lay their hands on the plunder.
Esther 9:6-10

The Jews could have taken revenge on those who meant to eradicate them. Though they did kill their enemies, they *never kept the spoil*. That point must be important, because the chapter repeats the fact over and over.

The Jews had every opportunity for personal gain. They could have used the power they had to make themselves richer, but they didn't. They could have brought further humiliation on the ones who wanted to kill them by plundering their homes, but they didn't. God wanted the Jews to protect themselves against those who meant to hurt them. He did not want them to get greedy or to act in vengeance.

Trusting God is an amazing thing when we are born again. Suddenly, we can trust God in everything- that includes not only physical needs, but also emotional ones. He is the source of all good things. If you trust in God, the grass on the other side becomes a lot less green, and you can find joy wherever you're at.

Sample prayer: *"Father, I choose to trust you today with all of my needs. Thank you for providing for me."*

Now Mordecai recorded these events, and he sent letters to all the Jews who lived in all the provinces of King Ahasuerus, both near and far, obliging them to celebrate the fourteenth day of the month of Adar, and the fifteenth day of the same month, annually, because on those days the Jews rid themselves of their enemies, and as the month which was turned for them from grief to joy and from mourning into a holiday; that they should make them days of feasting and rejoicing and sending choice portions of food to one another and gifts to the poor.

Esther 9:20-22

The act of celebration is one of the most exciting gifts God has given us. In the parable of the prodigal son, when the son returned home after leaving his father, his Father didn't punish him for his mistakes. He celebrated with a huge feast (Luke 15:11–32)!

"You turned my wailing into dancing; you removed my sackcloth and clothed me with joy."-*Psalm 30:11*

God doesn't want us to be serious and somber every time we come before Him, although there are occasions for that. When we begin to serve God, we are gifted with the ability to not focus solely on our circumstances; we can be joyful in what God has already given us! God wants you to be happy right where you're at- not just at your desired destination.

Ask God to help you believe in His promises. Whatever happens during the rest of your day, choose to celebrate because of the blessings you already have!

Sample prayer: *"Father, thank you for blessing me! Please give me a spirit of celebration today!"*

About the Author

K.J. Bryen is author of the devotional *Dare to be Brave: Devotionals from the stories of Gideon and Esther* and *Lokte*, a dark Christian thriller. *Lokte* was listed on Oklahoma's bestselling list for fictional books. She is a freelancer in her spare time at the Dog Dish Magazine, and wrote web content during her two years working at Oklahoma City's Fox 25/CW 34 television station. She has also done guest speaking engagements at the Chickasha Falling Leaves Author Festival and at the regional Independent Assembly of churches, and hosts regular book signing events across Oklahoma. She lives in Oklahoma City with her husband Adam and their two fur-babies, Houdini and Boo.